Test the Stuff You're Made Of

A Fun Little Book of Quizzes and Questions for Self-Discovery

my chaotic life

In a Word (or a Few)

Ever had trouble thinking of something to say when you've been asked to DESCRIBE YOURSELF? If so, this activity is for you! First CIRCLE all the words already listed here that DESCRIBE YOU. Then, as you DISCOVER NEW THINGS about yourself throughout this book, come back and ADD TO YOUR LIST. Now the next time someone asks about you, you won't be at a loss for words!

I am . . .

imaginative

giving

spiritual

helpful

cool

hopeful

creative

caring

practical

unique

bubbly

sweet

neat   confident   smart   outgoing

musical   memorable   loving   kind

humorous   shy   silly   understanding

playful   respectful   fun   athletic

popular   honest   talented   serious

social   strong   funny   colorful

loyal   witty

I am . . .

Your Room, Your World

It's no mystery that you can TELL PEOPLE ABOUT YOURSELF with words—but did you know that you can also express yourself *without* them? Sure! For example, your totally ORIGINAL FASHION SENSE and your GOOFY FACIAL EXPRESSIONS speak for you—and so does the state of your bedroom!

1. If you could paint your walls any color you want, you'd paint them
a. white, cream, beige—something very vanilla.
b. a super-bright color—like red, blue, or yellow.
c. a pretty pastel—maybe pink, lavender, or green.

2. When it's time for home-work, we'll find you
a. at your desk—every-thing you need is there.
b. flopped out on your bed—it's all about comfort.
c. in the kitchen—or *any* place besides your room!

3. When you go for clothes in your closet, you usually
a. reach in and pull out exactly what you wanted.
b. keep on rummaging until something suits your mood.
c. go fishing in search of something clean-ish.

4. When it comes to decorating your room, you're all for
a. framed artwork or movie prints.
b. photos of family and friends.
c. posters of all your fave celebs.

5. If you have girlfriends over to hang out, they'll be
a. in the kitchen or the den—wherever.
b. on your bed, making themselves at home
c. in your room, shoving stuff out of their way to make space to sit.

6. If you could relocate your bedroom to a new place, you'd move it to
a. an art museum.
b. a friend's house.
c. a shopping mall.

Continued on next page ➡

7. On an everyday basis, your bed looks like

a. ummmm . . . a bed? It has the basics—a no-nonsense pillow and blankets.

b. a mini petting zoo—it's covered in stuffed animals!

c. a magazine spread—it has a cool bedspread and fun pillows.

8. Walking into chez-you (um, that would be "your room") is like entering

a. a book store—it's no library, but it's got a pretty neat-and-tidy feel to it.

b. a rock concert—there are areas of calm, but then there's the closet!

c. a track-and-field event—hey, the obstacle course keeps it interesting.

How many

As ___ Bs ___ Cs ___

Scoring

If you answered mostly a's, your bedroom is a
PLACE OF PERFECTION.
You've got the goods on what it is to be on top of things. While your room
may not be as organized as, say, a librarian's bookcase, you *do* have
this fabulous habit of making a place for everything—and putting
everything in its place. Your room is the proof!

If you answered mostly b's, your bedroom is a
WELCOME RETREAT.
Your room is totally stuffed with things that just about scream
"Welcome!" Your room is all about favorite things—from familiar friends
to favorite memories. And the absolutely coolest thing about your room
is that you make your friends feel as comfy as you do there!

If you answered mostly c's, your bedroom is a
CREATIVE WORK-IN-PROGRESS.
You're way into changing things up to keep them fresh and interesting, and
your room totally reflects that. One day you're all about glittering things up;
the next, you've grabbed some toast to jam to some fave tunes. No matter
what your mood, your room is always so you!

Sleeping Beauty

Now that your bedroom is all talked
out, it's time to do some
SLEEP-TALKING. No need to shout
out random words in your deep
REM—the POSITION YOU SLEEP IN
reveals your personality. Really!
All you have to do is choose the description
that best explains your sleep position
to find out what your
SNOOZING STYLE has to
say about you.

On Your Back

In this position, you rest on your back. If you sleep with your arms close to your body, you're probably **QUIET** and **RESERVED**. And if you sleep with your arms stretched out, you're probably a very **GOOD LISTENER**.

Curled Up

In this position, you rest on your side with your knees pulled up to your chest. If you sleep curled up, you're probably a little bit on the **SHY** and **SENSITIVE** side. (Most American women sleep in this position!)

On Your Stomach

In this position, you rest flat on your belly with your arms up by your head. If you sleep on your stomach, you're probably **OUT-GOING** and maybe even **DARING!** (This is an unusual sleep position; only around 6.5% of Americans sleep on their stomachs.)

On Your Side

In this position, you rest on your side. If you sleep with your arms near your body, you're probably pretty **SOCIAL** and **EASY TO GET ALONG WITH**. But if you sleep in this position with your arms stretched out, it means something else: You may be **SLOW TO TRUST**.

Know Your Place

Did you know your BIRTH ORDER may influence your personality? If you have brothers or sisters, you've probably been compared to them time and time again. NOW IT'S YOUR TURN to do the comparing! For each list of traits, write a "1" next to items that apply more to you and a "o" next to things that apply more to them. (If you're an only child, compare yourself to your classmates instead.) Add up your totals to see if the order you were born in has affected YOUR PERSONALITY!

List A

You are more likely to . . .

_____ play by the rules or do what's expected of you
_____ be friendly and avoid "talking back"
_____ have drive and determination
_____ make better grades in school
_____ receive recognition for your skills or talents
_____ be chosen as a "leader"
_____ feel closer to your parents
_____ enjoy team sports (such as softball, soccer, or basketball)
_____ consider others' opinions when making a decision
_____ avoid forcefulness or aggression
_____ be social and have a lot of friends
_____ have your parents expect more from you
_____ have values similar to your parents'
_____ seek help or advice from others
_____ get nervous
_____ worry a lot

Total _____

List B

You are more likely to . . .

- ____ be more forceful or aggressive
- ____ believe things should be fair or equal
- ____ be independent
- ____ be popular
- ____ value your parents' opinions less
- ____ like individual sports (such as track, skating, or swimming)
- ____ get into trouble more
- ____ be more comfortable with total strangers
- ____ be attracted to risky activities, like roller coasters or extreme sports
- ____ talk less
- ____ avoid seeking help or advice from others
- ____ break the rules or do the opposite of what's expected of you
- ____ "get away" with more
- ____ have your parents be less strict with you
- ____ be more of a "loner"
- ____ receive less attention from your parents

Total _____

ADD IT UP!

Now total your score for each list; then compare the two. Is one total higher than the other, or are both scores pretty much the same? If you're an only child or the firstborn, your "List A" score will usually be higher than your "List B" score. And if you're the middle child, you'll probably share characteristics from both lists. If you're the youngest (or if you were born later but aren't the exact middle), your score for "List B" is likely to be higher.

Did your scores match your birth order placement?
YES   NO

Do you think having a step- or half-sibling makes a difference?

_____

_____

_____

Great Expectations

You've probably heard people say that they see "the glass" as half full or half empty. This test reveals the great mystery of how *you* see the glass—and more important, what exactly "the glass" has to do with anything!!!

CIRCLE YOUR ANSWERS

1. The recess bell rings. Your teacher waves you over. Think you're in trouble?
OH YEAH! **NOT REALLY**

2. Five minutes left to go in the game and your team is behind. Are you going to lose?
YOU BET **NO WAY**

3. Oh my—pop quiz! Will you ace it?
YES! **NO!**

4. You reveal your crush to your friends. They say your crush likes *you*. Believe it?
UH-HUH! **NUH-UH**

5. The weather forecast says rain, but the skies are sunny. Do you bring your umbrella?
OF COURSE **NAH**

For questions 1–2: Each no = 1 point
For questions 3–5: Each yes = 1 point

SCORE _____

If you scored 0–2, you see a
HALF-EMPTY GLASS.
So what does that mean? Well, basically it means you usually expect the worst. Oh great, just what you expected, right? But wait—being a *pessimist* isn't necessarily a bad thing! Having a "glass half empty" attitude helps you *prepare* for the worst. (See, that little gray rain cloud that follows you around *can* have a silver lining!)

If you scored 3–5, you see a
HALF-FULL GLASS.
In other words, you look at the bright side. And thinking positively can make the impossible possible! But there's one itty bitty little thing you should remember: Being an *optimist* doesn't mean you won't ever face disappointment. But your "glass half full" attitude will make disappointments easier to deal with!

Are You a Natural?

Some people are just BORN WITH TALENT (think Mozart, who started composing music when he was, what, just out of diapers?!). But other TALENTS CAN BE LEARNED—LIKE LEADERSHIP. With this test, you'll find out IF YOU'RE A LEADER. (Natch!)

1. You're on a class field trip—totally great, except for one small thing: You lost your class. You
a. look around for someone in uniform to help you find your group.
b. enjoy the freedom—you'll stumble across your classmates eventually.
c. freak out! Ohmigosh, how are you ever going to get back to school?!

2. You get in a huge blow-out with your parental units. When it's over, you
a. ask the 'rents what you can do to make things right.
b. pretend everything's okay, even though you're still upset.
c. stomp your feet, slam some doors, and let them know everything's not okay.

3. Your parents go all cool and let you choose how to spend your vacation. You
a. pack your bags for camp—think of all the great stuff you'll experience!
b. plan a fam vacation—summer wouldn't be the same without one.
c. look forward to vegging out at home, hanging by the pool and watching TV.

4. Your best friend agrees with you on most things. When she doesn't, you
a. put on a broken record, telling her again and again why you're right.
b. put on a mask, pretending to agree with her but secretly believing you're right.
c. put on a new hat, agreeing with her because she must be right!

5. Your future is out there—from colleges to cars. You think
a. it's in the bag: You determine your own fate.
b. it's negotiable: You'll work it out with destiny.
c. it's a big question mark: It's all about fate!

Scoring

How many

As ___ Bs ___ Cs ___

If you answered mostly a's, you **LEAD NATURALLY.** Girl, you've got it down! This leadership stuff comes easily to you; from first-class communication skills to oodles of confidence, you know what it takes. You're probably already a leader in your friends' eyes. What's next—your class, your country, the world?!

If you answered mostly b's, you **LEAD WHEN NEEDED.** Sure, you know *how* to lead, you're just not so sure you should be the one doing it. Following is perfectly okay; but if you want to gain more confidence in your leadership abilities, try volunteering to represent your class for a group project or help out in the community!

If you answered mostly c's, you **FOLLOW THE LEADER.** Leadership skills can be learned, if you're interested in switching sides. But don't be so quick to discount your role as a follower. After all, without followers, the world would be like a big game of *Survivor* but without any winners.

Win, Win, Win!

It takes a little competitive spirit to be a success—and only a little more to drive your friends crazy. What's your attitude about competition?

1. 'Fess up: Have you ever quit a game because you weren't winning?
YEAH   NAH

2. Do you get a little thrill out of being the first one to finish tests or class assignments?
YEAH   NAH

3. Would it bum you out if your teach congratulated your BFF on a test, but not you?
SURE   NOT REALLY

4. Ever tried to prove that you're more into your fave celebs than your friends are?
OH YEAH   NOT ME

5. Do you really, really, really want to make better grades than your friends do?
YUP   NOPE

6. Is it an absolute must that you have more stylish clothes than your friends do?
WAY   NO WAY

7. Do you have a sibling or a friend whom you just hafta outdo—no matter what?
UH-HUH   NUH-UH

Scoring

Count up the number of your "yes" answers.

SCORE _____

| 1 | 2 | 3 | 4 | 5 | 6 | 7 |

Less Competitive

More Competitive

If you answered "yes" to 0–2 questions, you're a **SPORT.** Having fun and *getting along* are way, way, waaay more important to you than winning. Your friends probably really love that you're game for just playing.

If you answered "yes" to 3–5 questions, you're a **COMPETITOR.** You play hard—in the classroom, on the field, or any other time. But you're a pretty quick study at figuring out how to keep the "fun" in games all the same.

If you answered "yes" to 6–7 questions, you're a **CONTENDER.** Your competitive drive is in a little thing we like to call "overdrive." In other words, you play *only* to win. Ready for a new challenge? Be the best friend you can be!

Pure Perfection

Have you been SWEATIN' YOUR SCORES on the quizzes in this book? (Even a little itty bit?) Take this quiz to determine just how much PRESSURE YOU PUT ON YOURSELF to be perfect.

1. You're jotting down a note to a friend when you notice—gasp!—you misspelled her name. You
a. get angry with yourself for making such a silly mistake.
b. crumple up the note and begin again with an exasperated sigh.
c. laugh it off, fix the error, and keep on writing.

2. Your teacher scribbles comments all over your paper. You
a. are not-so-happy with yourself—obviously, you need a lot of improvement.
b. are happy for your teacher's help—her comments will set you on the right track.
c. aren't bugged—it's pretty clear your teacher is being way too picky.

3. You get a gift certificate for your b-day and decided to put it away for a rainy day. You'll find it again
a. easily—you're very, very organized.
b. with a little effort—it's in one of a couple of spots.
c. only after you hire a search-and-rescue crew.

4. Your homework is to come up with a short personal motto. You choose:
a. Always be the best.
b. Always do your best.
c. Accept yourself.

5. You're having friends over for a sleepover. To get ready, you
a. clean up your room and make it pretty.
b. kick any bedroom clutter under your bed.
c. relax—your friends won't care if things aren't tidy.

6. The lowest grade you'd feel okay about bringing home is
a. an A+.
b. a B+.
c. a C+.

How many

_____ **As x 4** = _____

_____ **Bs x 2** = _____

_____ **Cs x 0** = _____

TOTAL SCORE _____

If your score is 16–24, you
REQUIRE PERFECTION.
Wow. You really expect a lot from yourself, and not just on school days—on holidays and weekends too! Everybody makes mistakes—yes, even *you!* Do the right thing: Cut yourself a little slack from time to time.

If your score is 8–14, you
WANT PERFECTION.
Yeah, it's true: You've set some pretty high standards for yourself. But you've also figured out when it's okay to relax those oh-so-high expectations. Allowing yourself to make mistakes feels good, and you know it!

If your score is 0–6, you
ACCEPT PERFECTION.
Forget your homework? No problem. Trip up the stairs? No biggie. You're cool with just being you—when you're perfect and when you're not. Your attitude makes it easy for you to deal with, well, anything at all!

The Chance Dance

With every decision you make, you dance around opportunities. Answer these questions to find out more about how the choices you make affect your choreography.

1.
If you're out skateboarding or biking, are you wearing a helmet?
OF COURSE   NO

2.
If there's a tree or a jungle gym in sight, are you climbing it?
WAY   NO WAY

3.
If you're riding in a car, are you wearing a seatbelt?
ALWAYS   NEVER

4.
If someone double-dog dared you, would you sit next to your crush on the school bus?
YEAH   NAH

5.
If your friend's parents said lights out at 10 o'clock, would you stay up later?
YUP   NOPE

6.
If NASA offered you a free ride, would you be on the next space shuttle?
UH-HUH   NUH-UH

7.
If you had a chance to share your talent on TV, would you?
SURE   NO!

Scoring

For questions 1 and 3:
Each "no" = 1 point
For questions 2, 4, 5, 6, and 7:
Each "yes" = 1 point

SCORE _____

If you scored 0–3, you're a **SLOW DANCER.** Chances are you like the slower, safer pace of swaying to a favorite song. And that's all good. But if you really want to rock out to some fast songs and fear is stopping you from showing off your dance moves, don't let the safety net you cast around yourself stop you.

If you scored 4–7, you're a **FAST DANCER.** Chances are, dance music is your thing—and we're not talking about the fox trot. The envy of other disco-goers, you love shakin' your groove. But don't get so distracted by the fun that you forget to watch out for spills on the dance floor—being happy is cool, but so is being *safe!*

Creative Cat

There are all sorts of **CREATIVE FOLKS** in the world—musicians, artists, actors, comedians, writers, and you! Take this quiz to find out what kind of **CREATIVE CAT** you are!

1. Think fast! You can be anything for a day; you choose to be
a. your adorable pet (duh!).
b. a pop star—definitely, a pop star.
c. someone really, really smart, like an author.
d. a modern-day Van Gogh—with both ears intact!

2. It's all icky and gloomy outside, so to pass the time you
a. nap, nap, nap.
b. surf the 'net.
c. read a book.
d. doodle away.

3. Pizza or tacos? The decision is yours. You

a. say, "eenie, meenie, minie, moe . . ."
b. ask someone else to choose.
c. listen to your cravings.
d. carefully weigh the benefits of each.

4. Your oh-so-lovely artistic creations end up

a. where all good art goes to rest (under the bed).
b. wherever there are magnets, like on the fridge.
c. with your photos, memory books, and stuff like that.
d. just about everywhere—you can't help but see them!

5. You'd much rather spend your free afternoons

a. in front of the TV.
b. in the great outdoors.
c. anywhere with your friends!
d. in a crafter's studio!

How many

As __ Bs __ Cs __ Ds __

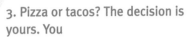

Scoring

Each a = 0 points   Each b = 1 point
Each c = 2 points   Each d = 3 points

SCORE _____

If you scored 0–6 points, you're an
ENTERTAINING CAT.

You soak up entertainment more quickly than you can find it on the 'net! Movies, music, TV—it's all you. You express your creativity by being in on what's hot in the world of entertainment!

If you scored 7–11 points, you're a
STORYTELLING CAT.

You love, love, love a good story. You express your creativity through storytelling, reading, and gossiping with the girls. Any which way, it's very rare for you to ever be bored!

If you scored 12–15 points, you're a
CRAFTY CAT.

You express your creativity through arts and crafts. From fine-art projects to scrapbook pages, you love seeing things from your imagination come to life, again and again!

Penny for Your Thoughts?

Okay, just in case you're all quizzed out, we're going to do another kind of activity. No worries—it still shows what you're made of, just in a totally different way.

For this activity, hunt out a comfy, cozy spot where nobody will bother you (at least for a little while). Now, when you're all settled in, start writing. Here's the kind of strange part: You're not going to write a story or a note—or even sentences. You're just going to jot down every single word that comes to mind. No, really! Don't edit yourself or try to make the words make sense—just write them down. Then, once you've filled these pages, don't look at what you've written for several days.

....

....

....

....

....

....

....

....

....

....

....

....

....

....

....

....

....

Welcome back! (Is it really several days later, or are you peeking ahead?!)
Are you ready for the next step? Go back and reread what you wrote.
Huh? That's it? Yup. You may be surprised . . .

So, now that you've read your words, whaddya think they mean? Can you tell what you were thinking when you did the exercise—or who or what was on your mind? *Free association* (writing or speaking words as they come to you, without structure) sometimes reveals things that are on your mind *even when you don't realize they are.* Kinda cool, huh? Free association can help you get to know yourself better. And you know what the best part is? You can do it anywhere, any time!

A and B Personalities
Which R U?

Being an "A" personality has nothing to do with the grades you make—it's about the way you REACT TO THE WORLD AROUND YOU! There are TWO "TYPES" OF PEOPLE in the world: Type A and Type B. Take this quiz to find out which type you are!

ONE

Your mom is making lunch, and you ask her to cut off the crusts from your PB&J. But when she presents your plate, the crusts are still there. Do you refuse to eat the sandwich until the crusts are gone?
YES   NO

TWO

You're dying to talk to your BFF, but her line is busy! Do you keep dialing until you get through?
YES   NO

THREE

Your dad is supposed to pick you up after school, but you've been waiting FOREVER. When he finally shows up—half an hour late—what do you say to him?
a. Nothing. You're so angry, if you said "hello," you'd breathe fire!
b. "Hey, Dad! What's up?"
c. "Um, Dad, thanks for picking me up and everything, but do you know you were supposed to be here half an hour ago?"

FOUR

You did the best in your class on a test, but you didn't get 100%. Do you wish you'd done better?
YES   NO

FIVE

You're hanging out at the park with some friends when someone suggests shooting hoops. The pick-up basketball game is just for fun, without prizes at stake. Do you get upset if your team doesn't win?
YES   NO

SIX

Are you one of those people who is absolutely never ever late?

YES   **NO**

SEVEN

You found an awesome gift for your friend's birthday. But when you hear about the gift someone else bought, suddenly yours doesn't sound so great. Do you buy something else?

YES   **NO**

EIGHT

School work, after-school activities, time with friends, and family stuff have left you really tired. What do you do?

a. Keep on going—there's no time to take a break!

b. Take a rest from all the activity for a little while and just chill.

c. Turn down a couple of invites, but still keep some activities on your social calendar.

NINE

Worry much about grades?

YES   **NO**

TEN

You just found out that your teacher next year is all about assigning "group work" in class, and you will be doing a lot of projects this year with your classmates. Would you prefer to work alone?

YES   **NO**

Scoring

A or B?

Turn the page to find out your score—and discover more about your personality!

A and B Personalities
C Your Score

Use the space below to SCORE YOUR RESPONSES from the previous pages. For the "yes or no" questions, give yourself 10 points for every "yes" answer and "0" for every "no." For the multiple-choice questions, give yourself 10 points for each "A," 0 points for each "B," and 5 points for each "C." Then ADD UP THE TOTAL SCORE and find your results!

1. _____

2. _____

3. _____

4. _____

5. _____

6. _____

7. _____

8. _____

9. _____

10. _____

Total: _____

SCORES

0–49 = Type B personality   50–100 = Type A personality

Note: If your score is in the middle range (40–60), you share characteristics of both personality types.

Type A

Remember when we said that just because you made straight A's didn't mean that you were a Type A? Well, that was sort of true . . . and sort of not. The thing is, Type A personalities are waaay into achievement. They're totally driven to make good grades, win at games, and generally be the best at everything they possibly can. That's great because it means they've got goals and they're constantly challenging themselves. But if you're a Type A personality, the constant pressure to succeed borders on an attempt to be just too-too perfect. So sometimes somebody has to remind the Type A to close her eyes, take a deep breath, and just relax. Achievement comes easily; resting is the hardest thing for a Type A personality to do!

Type B

Like Type A personalities, Type B's can be good students; but if they make a less-than-perfect grade here and there, it doesn't bug them out. In fact, when it comes down to it, not much of anything stresses out a Type B! Type B personalities like to win, but they don't get way upset if they lose. They don't have a problem just chillin' and kickin' it with friends—even when they have homework to do! And if someone tells them to take a break, they're on it like glaze on a doughnut. Sometimes B types can be so laid back they're in danger of falling over; then they just need a little push in the other direction to straighten themselves out. But generally, this go-with-the-flow attitude is a healthy way to deal with everyday life!

Is That a Model in the Mirror?

Models come in all shapes, sizes, and ages. The one thing they have in common is this super-cool confidence about the way they look. This test takes a good look at your model readiness!

1. A friend tells you you're looking so very cute today. You
   a. say thanks.
   b. say it's not true.

2. You could be talked into exercising or playing sports if you knew
   a. they'd make you healthy and strong.
   b. they'd make your body look absolutely perfect!

3. School pictures are, well, school pictures. When the time comes, you've learned to
   a. smile for the camera.
   b. grin and bear it.

4. Potato chips, ice cream, chocolate—oh joy! You get the munchies when
   a. your tummy is doing the "hungry, hungry, hungry" chant.
   b. you're so bored you just hafta do *something*.

5. You arrive at a pool party and you're totally ready to
   a. splash in the pool! What else? You and your bathing suit are ready.
   b. hang out with friends—but not without your towel or a T-shirt.

Scoring

Total up the number of times you answered "a" and the number of times you answered "b."

As ____   Bs ____

If you answered mostly a's, you're
CATWALK CONFIDENT.
Being Catwalk Confident doesn't mean that you don't sometimes wonder if you're pretty enough or thin enough (we all wonder!). But overall, you are perfectly content with your-self—which gives you confidence in the way you look.

If you answered mostly b's, you're
MIRROR AVOIDANT.
Who's that pretty girl in the mirror there? It's you! Surprised? When you take a long look in the mirror, the first things you see are the things you don't like. Why not take another close look— we bet you could make a list of things you do like, as well. Try it!

Your Style

Fashion sense is one thing; learning style is another entirely. Bet you didn't know that you pick up information differently than your friends do. It's true! Need proof? Take this test!

1. No one loves memorizing vocabulary, but it sure is easier if
a. you hear the words spoken out loud.
b. you write out the words 10 times each.
c. you can see the words written down.

2. Your friend is reading a book she can't stop talking about. You
a. listen to her as she rambles off all the exciting details.
b. ask to borrow the book when she's done so you can read it.
c. think it'd make a great movie—one that you'd go see for sure!

3. You'd go back to preschool again, but only if you were bribed with
a. story time.
b. finger painting.
c. show and tell.

4. Science class isn't half bad when you get to
a. listen to a guest speaker.
b. experiment in the lab.
c. watch some sort of film.

5. You have absolutely no clue where you're going. You
a. try to find someone to give you directions.
b. ask someone to lead you there.
c. keep your eyes peeled for someone with a map.

6. You're totally not a fraidy cat—except when it comes to
a. ghost stories!
b. haunted houses!
c. horror movies!

Scoring

Add up how many responses you had for each category: a, b, and c. Which letter did you answer most?

As ____

Bs ____

Cs ____

(Note: If you didn't choose one letter more than the others, then you use a combination of learning styles. Read the descriptions for any letters you chose more than once.)

If you have mostly a's, you learn by **LISTENING**. You have an auditory learning style, so stuff sticks best in that lovely brain of yours if you hear it. If you're into trying to remember things better, try making tapes or reading out loud!

If you have mostly b's, you learn by **DOING**. You have a tactile learning style, which means hands-on activities are your ultimate brain food. Want a trick to remember better? Try acting out vocab words and historic events!

If you have mostly c's, you learn by **SEEING**. You have a visual learning style, so your brain is crammed with images. Want in on a secret? If you close your eyes when trying to remember, you can picture what you learned!

Taking Sides

Sometimes you're right and sometime you're . . . left.
Right- or left-brained, that is. Take this test to get a
ONE-SIDED EXPLANATION of your BRAIN ACTIVITY!

1. School uniforms—yuck! If you have to wear one, you'll
a. change it up somehow to make it one-of-a-kind.
b. start a petition to change the uniform policy.

2. To convince your parents you'd be a responsible pet owner, you're saving money
a. by spending less on clothes. (Or maybe CDs. Or movies.)
b. by putting away a percentage of your allowance every week.

3. You're giving your friend directions to your place. You
a. show her where to go by drawing a map.
b. tell her where to go by writing out directions.

4. Your BFF's birthday is next week. You've decided to
a. paint a picture frame for her with a funky, fun design.
b. make her a CD with songs you know she loves.

5. For your homework, you've been given a drawing to color. You
a. do your own thing.
b. color inside the lines.

6. Your friends wanna play Calvin-ball, but it's new to you. You
a. leap right in, ready to learn.
b. hang back and watch at first.

7. You're sitting down to dinner with the fam. As usual, you
a. sculpt your food, pushing it around your plate.
b. clear your plate, one forkful at a time.

8. Your friends are planning a surprise going-away party for your favorite teacher ever. You volunteer to
a. make the decorations—you've already got some great ideas!
b. choose the music—you know you can find the perfect party songs!

9. Your friends all think you've got an oh-so-impressive
a. way with words.
b. way with numbers.

Count up the number of "a" answers and the number of "b" answers.

Scoring

How many
As ___ Bs ___

If you chose mostly a's, you're
RIGHT-BRAINED.

Right-Brainers are super-creative. You don't follow the rules so much as make up your own! You're in it for the "big picture," and you don't really want to bother with details. Oh yeah, and you tend to be pretty tuned in to your emotions too!

If you chose mostly b's, you're
LEFT-BRAINED.

Left-Brainers are math people. And science people. And music people too! Basically, you like doing stuff where you get to dive into all the nitty-gritty details. And unlike the Right-Brainers, you are more into facts and figures than feelings.

Sorting Through Friendships

This ultra-unique activity compares the way you see yourself to the way your friends see you.

First you'll need 25 note cards. (Feel free to cut a few sheets of paper down to playing-card size instead.) On each note card, write down one of the phrases from these pages. When your cards are complete, turn the page.

1. I expect a lot of myself.
2. I get embarrassed easily.
3. I get angry with myself when I mess up.
4. I question whether I'm pretty.
5. I have friends who make me feel good about myself.
6. I sometimes lose my temper when I'm angry.
7. Any troubles I have, I probably caused.
8. I don't always trust super-friendly people.
9. I am responsible.
10. I am a hard worker.
11. It's easy for me to keep myself in check.
12. I am somewhat disorganized.
13. I like to express myself and my emotions.
14. I don't care about a lot of stuff.
15. I am positive.
16. I try not to think about my problems too much.
17. I like the way I look.
18. I am shy.
19. Most people who know me like me.
20. I don't like to get into big arguments.
21. Once I make up my mind, I stick to it.
22. I have a hard time making decisions.
23. I act spontaneously, without planning.
24. I'm scared of telling people what I want.
25. There are many things I'd like to achieve in life.

Sorting the Cards

Take the cards and sort them into seven different piles in order, from the least like you (pile #1) to the most like you (pile #7). When you're done sorting the cards, write down the numbers of the phrases you placed in each pile using the space below.

1	2	3	4	5	6	7

Resorting the Cards

Now take the cards and sort them again. This time, sort them according to the person you would *like* to be, with the phrases least like the person you would like to be in the first pile and those most like who you want to be in the last pile. When you're finished, record your results.

1	2	3	4	5	6	7

Are the two piles different? In what way? What does this tell you about who you'd like to become?

....

....

....

You: Reflected in Friendship

Now invite a friend to sort the cards. Ask her to place them in the piles according to the way she sees you. (But don't let her know how you've sorted the cards!) When she has finished, record her results here:

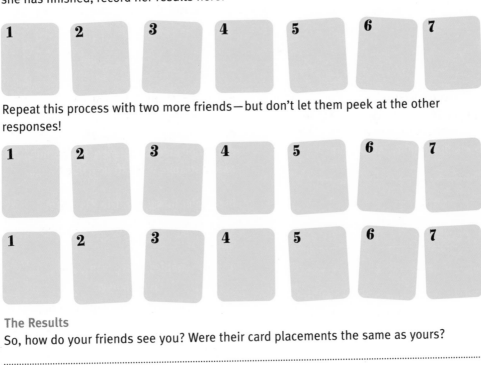

1	2	3	4	5	6	7

Repeat this process with two more friends—but don't let them peek at the other responses!

1	2	3	4	5	6	7

1	2	3	4	5	6	7

The Results

So, how do your friends see you? Were their card placements the same as yours?

....

....

....

The Big 5

This book is full of all kinds of tests that reveal just about everything you could want to know about your personality! But some researchers believe you can find out everything (yes, *everything!*) about a person's personality from just five categories, called "The Big 5."

Think you can sort all your personality traits into just five categories? Use the space below to take a guess at what The Big 5 personality factors are.

_____

_____

_____

_____

_____

Did you make your guesses? All right, here's the real answer. The Big 5 are
1. Openness to Experience
2. Conscientiousness
3. Extraversion
4. Agreeableness
5. Emotional Stability

What?! Yeah, that's kind of what we thought. After all, these words don't describe anyone we know. But maybe that's because researchers have some pretty strange ways to describe things.

In simpler language, The Big 5 are

1. How willing a person is to try new things or **EXPLORE DIFFERENT IDEAS**

2. How reliable, trustworthy, and **DEPENDABLE** a person is

3. How **OUTGOING OR SHY** a person is

4. How a person **GETS ALONG** with others

5. How a person **REACTS EMOTIONALLY** to people and situations

In the next five quizzes, you'll get to test yourself on The Big 5. But to make it more fun, we've changed things up a little bit—so instead of just finding out if you're more or less extraverted, you'll also find out what kind of butterfly you are!

One of the coolest things about The Big 5 is that your test results don't change much over time. So if you take these five quizzes again in 1 year, 5 years, or even 20 years, your answers are likely to be almost exactly the same!

Here's what's to come:

What Kind of Butterfly Are You? measures Extraversion.

Hey, Hey! What Do You Say? measures Agreeableness.

Miss Independent measures Conscientiousness.

Stress Case measures Emotional Stability.

Active Imagination measures Openness to Experience.

Oh yeah, one more thing. Before you take these tests, you have to take a special pledge. (For real.) Repeat after us: "There are no wrong answers." That's all.

You've taken the pledge, now don't go trying to answer the questions the way you think you should—just answer honestly.

Pencils ready? Go!

Continued on next page ➡

What Kind of Butterfly Are You?

Some butterflies are SO BRIGHT AND COLORFUL that you can't help but notice them against a landscape. Others are colored in a way that they BLEND INTO THEIR SURROUNDINGS. **Which kind of butterfly are you?**

Rate each of the words below according to how well it describes you. If something is just not you, score it a 1. If it's neither like nor unlike you, score it a 5. And if it's totally you, score it a 9.

A. Talkative ___

B. Shy ___

C. Friendly ___

D. Quiet ___

E. Bold ___

F. Timid ___

G. Energetic ___

H. Reserved ___

Scoring

For items A, C, E, and G, the number you assigned is your final score. For items B, D, F, and H, you'll subtract your number from 10 to get a final score. Add all the scores together for your total.

A. ____

B. 10 – ____ = ____

C. ____

D. 10 – ____ = ____

E. ____

F. 10 – ____ = ____

G. ____

H. 10 – ____ = ____

Total ____

If your total is 8–29, you're a **NATURAL BUTTERFLY.**
Parties, big crowds, lots of people—so you, right? Nah, we didn't think so. Natural Butterflies are a little bit shy, so you're much more at home in places with less noise and fewer people. (Natural Butterflies are also called "introverts.")

If your total is 30–49, you're a **SEASONAL BUTTERFLY.**
Now we see you, now we don't! Seasonal butterflies tend to fly in and out of the social scene, depending on their mood. You like people and everything, but you also like time alone. (Seasonal Butterflies are also called "ambiverts.")

If your total is 50–72, you're a **SOCIAL BUTTERFLY.**
Hello, Social Butterfly! You just love taking center stage and talk-talk-talking—wherever, whenever! Parties? Crowds? Adventures? Bring it on! You're happiest when surrounded by people. (Social butterflies are also called "extraverts.")

Hey, Hey! What Do You Say?

Okay, we all have FAVORITE SAYINGS—from celebrity quotes to inside jokes with our crew. The words that slip out of your mouth tell the outside world a lot about you . . . including your FUTURE CAREER CALLING!

Rate each of the sayings below according to how likely you are to say it (or something like it). If you would never, ever say it, score it a 1. If you might sometimes use the saying, score it a 5. And if it's very much something you'd say, score it a 9.

A. I couldn't care less. _____

D. I'm glad we're friends. _____

E. I don't have time for this. _____

F. I'm so proud of you! _____

B. I'm listening. _____

G. You're getting on my nerves. _____

C. Whatever. _____

H. Let's try to work together. _____

Next write the numbers you assigned in the blank spaces below. For items A, C, E, and G, you'll subtract your number from 10 to get a final score. For items B, D, F, and H, the number you assigned is your final score. Add all the final scores together for your total.

A. 10 – ____ = ____

B. ____

C. 10 – ____ = ____

D. ____

E. 10 – ____ = ____

F. ____

G. 10 – ____ = ____

H. ____

Total ____

If your total is 8–29, you're **MYSTERIOUS.**

Mysterious personalities are not always good about showing emotions (they might reveal too much!). But you *are* good at calmly dealing with facts. As a Mysterious personality, you might make a good detective, researcher, or computer programmer.

If your total is 30–49, you're **FRIENDLY.**

We wouldn't say Friendly people are all about other people's emotions and needs, but they sure do care about others and get along with them easily. Friendly personalities are great teammates, so careers in sales or marketing are a great match!

If your total is 50–72, you're **WELCOMING.**

Welcoming personalities are just that: Welcoming! Kind, caring, and cooperative, you are always there to listen to others or lend a helping hand. Welcoming personalities are great in "caring" jobs—like nursing, counseling, or volunteer work.

Miss Independent

You depend on your family, you depend on your friends, but
DO YOU DEPEND ON YOURSELF?

Rate each of the words below according to how well it describes you. If something is just not you, score it a 1. If it's neither like nor unlike you, score it a 5. And if it's totally you, score it a 9.

A. Disorganized

_____

B. Sloppy

_____

C. Inefficient

_____

D. Careless

_____

E. Orderly

_____

F. Efficient

_____

G. Consistent

_____

H. Practical

_____

Scoring

For items A, B, C, and D, you'll subtract your number from 10 to get a final score. For items E, F, G, and H, the number you assigned is your final score. Add all the final scores together for your total.

A. 10 –____ = ____
B. 10 –____ = ____
C. 10 –____ = ____
D. 10 –____ = ____
E. ____
F. ____
G. ____
H. ____
Total ____

If your total is 8–29, you're **MISS UNPREDICTABLE.**
Um, it's probably no news to you that your room isn't always picked up, you're not always on time for dinner, and you sometimes forget to do your homework. It's safe to say, you get along with a little help from your friends!

If your total is 30–49, you're **MISS INTERDEPENDENT.**
You've got your own way of organizing your time and responsibilities—and most of the time, it totally works. But since there are times when the phone seems more important than homework, you still need your friends to keep you in line!

If your total is 50–72, you're **MISS INDEPENDENT.**
Nobody needs to remind you to do your homework or send out your party invitations on time—you just do it. You can depend on yourself, which means others can depend on you too—like your good friend Miss Unpredictable!

Stress Case

UGH! The dog got into the trash, your sister read your diary, and you've got more homework than you know what to do with.
HOW DO *YOU* REACT?

Rate each of the words below according to how well it describes you. If something is just not you, score it a 1. If it's neither like nor unlike you, score it a 5. And if it's totally you, score it a 9.

A. Trusting

———

B. Even-Tempered

———

C. Mellow

———

D. Relaxed

———

E. Jealous

———

F. Sensitive

———

G. Moody

———

H. Nervous

———

For items A, B, C, and D, the number you assigned is your final score. For items E, F, G, and H, you'll be subtracting your number from 10 to get a final score. Add all the final scores together for your total.

A. ____

B. ____

C. ____

D. ____

E. 10 – ____ = ____

F. 10 – ____ = ____

G. 10 – ____ = ____

H. 10 – ____ = ____

Total ____

If your score is 8–29, you're a **DIVA.**
Um, you know those stories you hear about celebs who get ultra-upset when they're stressed? Well, that's not you—but it could be. We know sometimes it just feels right to cry and yell (it's good to let it out!), but sometimes *talking* helps too.

If your score is 30–49, you're a **PRINCESS.**
Sometimes you get stressed and you remain perfectly composed, just like your mum the Queen. But it's tough not to give in to a good sniffle fit now and then. When you *do* react with tears and tissues, try breathing deeply and phoning a friend.

If your score is 50–72, you're a **QUEEN.**
Yeah, yeah, we know—there are times when you want to kick and scream about the unfairness of, well, life. But the thing is . . . you don't. You calm yourself down when you recognize that the stress is only temporary. How very regal!

Active Imagination?

Are your FEET PLACED FIRMLY ON THE GROUND—or do your daydreams lift you up, UP, AND INTO THE CLOUDS?

Rate each of the words below according to how well it describes you. If something is just not you, score it a 1. If it's neither like nor unlike you, score it a 5. And if it's totally you, score it a 9.

A. Simple

——

B. Opinionated

——

C. Creative

——

D. Imaginative

——

E. Average

——

F. Ordinary

——

G. Deep

——

H. Intellectual

——

Scoring

For items A, B, E, and F, you'll subtract your number from 10 to get a final score. For items C, D, G, and H, the number you assigned is your final score. Add all the final scores together for your total.

A. 10 – ____ = ____

B. 10 – ____ = ____

C. ____

D. ____

E. 10 – ____ = ____

F. 10 – ____ = ____

G. ____

H. ____

Total ____

If your score is 8–29, your imagination is **FEET ON THE GROUND.**

Your daydreams keep things firmly grounded in reality—your reality. People and places you know are totally your bag. And most of the time, you'll say "pass" to new foods, places, or experiences.

If your score is 30–49, your imagination is **HEAD IN THE CLOUDS.**

You won't get totally bored with going places you know and doing things that you've done before. But you do let your imagination drift to distant lands (and handsome foreign princes!).

If your score is 50–72, your imagination is **FEET IN THE CLOUDS.**

Your imagination takes you on out-of-this-world adventures. And it's hard for you *not* to think about all the things you'd like to see, learn, and do in the great big world out there!

Temperaments

Okay, now that you've got The Big 5 down, are you ready for The Big 4? Just kidding! Well, sort of. Actually, there are researchers who think personality can be grouped into four categories, but the four categories are called "temperaments."

You're a smart girl. Knowing what you do about The Big 5, can you guess what these four personality measures are? Try writing your guesses below.

_____

_____

_____

_____

Give up? It was kind of a trick question. (Sorry!) The four temperament categories aren't the same as the Big 5. They're

1. Extraversion-Introversion
2. Sensing-Intuition
3. Thinking-Feeling
4. Judging-Perceiving

Just as with The Big 5, researchers believe every person has a little bit of each of these factors—but in a different combination. You've probably already figured out the only obvious similarity between the temperaments and The Big 5 is extraversion—but even that's different! The Big 5 measures extraversion according to how much you like to be around others, and

this temperament sorter seeks to discover if you become *energized* by other people.

In the next four quizzes, you'll get to test yourself on the four temperaments. But to keep things interesting, we've changed the tests just a wee bit.

DO YOU GET ENOUGH "ME" TIME? measures Extraversion-Introversion.

ATTENTION! measures Sensing-Intuition.

DO YOU FOLLOW YOUR HEART? measures Thinking-Feeling.

WHO DOES THE WORLD SEE? measures Judging-Perceiving.

After taking all four tests, you'll discover a unique letter combo (such as INTP or ESFJ) that describes you. The letter grouping is a bunch of gobbledy-gook to most folks, but give those letters to researchers (or search for them on the Internet), and you'll be surprised at how much they reveal!

Now remember—there are *no* wrong answers! Turn the page to begin . . .

Some people get totally pumped from being around people; others get exhausted. Do you know which type you are?

Do You Get Enough "Me" Time?

For each question, check the phrase that fits you best from either Column A or Column B. If both answers describe you, choose the answer that makes you more comfortable.

Column A

1. I'm totally cool if I'm around crowds and noise. ❏
2. I like to talk a lot. ❏
3. I want everyone to know if I'm excited! ❏
4. Sometimes I just blurt things out. ❏
5. I get bored very easily—I can't stand to do nothing. ❏
6. In class, I like to work in groups. ❏
7. I'm perfectly comfortable being the center of attention. ❏

Column B

1. I'm into quiet places without a lot of people. ❏
2. I'd rather listen than talk. ❏
3. If I'm excited, I keep it to myself. ❏
4. I always think before I speak. ❏
5. I like having time alone to just chill and relax. ❏
6. In class, I like working independently. ❏
7. I'm perfectly content watching from the sidelines. ❏

Scoring

If you checked more Column A responses, you're **"E," FOR EXTRAVERTED.**
E's get energized being around people, which means you don't need a whole lotta "me time." In fact, if you spend too much time alone, it can make you feel kinda tired and blue. To keep up your energy level, make time for friends—even if that means doing homework together.

If you checked more Column B responses, you're **"I," FOR INTROVERTED.**
Parties, study groups, babysitting— nothing is more exhausting for an **I** than being around people. The way you get your energy is by spending time alone. Being introverted doesn't have to mean being antisocial, but it does mean penciling in "me time" to keep you energized!

Attention!

This quiz reveals what kind of information really grabs your attention.

For each question, check the phrase that better describes you from either Column A or Column B. If both answers fit you, choose the one that feels more comfortable.

Column A

1. I learn stuff by watching or doing. ❑
2. I'd rather know what's real than what's possible. ❑
3. I usually give specific, very detailed descriptions. ❑
4. I like to think things through practically. ❑
5. My experience helps me make choices. ❑
6. I like doing things the way I'm used to. ❑
7. Common sense is more important than imagination. ❑

Column B

1. I learn stuff best through explanation. ❑
2. Possibilities are more important than reality. ❑
3. I explain things by comparing them to other things. ❑
4. I like to use my imagination to solve problems. ❑
5. My instincts help me make decisions. ❑
6. I like trying new ways to do things. ❑
7. Having an imagination is more important than being practical. ❑

Scoring

If you checked more Column A responses, you're an **"S," OR A SENSOR.**
S's are interested in stuff they can sense. To you, seeing, hearing, tasting, smelling, and touching are the best ways to gather info. You trust your sensory experiences more than anything!

If you checked more Column B responses, you're an **"N," OR AN INTUITOR.**
N's don't care so much about thing they can taste or hear or see—they want to know about the things they can't sense. You love following up on a hunch or going with your "gut" feeling!

Do You Follow Your Heart or Your Head?

Are you full of heart—or is it logic that leads you?

For each question, check the phrase that better describes you from either Column A or Column B. If both answers fit you, go with the one that naturally draws you first.

Column A

1. It's important for people to tell the truth. ❑
2. I always question what people tell me. ❑
3. Other people's opinions are often wrong. ❑
4. I think the world should always run on logic. ❑
5. I consider both the good and the bad features of my choices. ❑
6. I notice when other people mess up. ❑
7. It's okay if people occasionally ask me how I'm feeling. ❑

Column B

1. It's important for everyone to get along. ❑
2. I always believe what others tell me. ❑
3. It's worth listening to other people. ❑
4. I believe the world should pay attention to individuals. ❑
5. I wonder about how my choices will affect other people. ❑
6. I like to make other people happy. ❑
7. I really appreciate it when people ask how I'm feeling. ❑

Scoring

If you checked more Column A responses, you're a **"T," OR A THINKER.**
T is for Thinker, but that doesn't make you smarter than the Feelers. It does mean that you trust facts over feelings—which is why you're more likely to follow your head than your heart.

If you checked more Column B responses, you're an **"F," OR A FEELER.**
F's are *very* in tune to emotions—their own, their friends', even those of perfect strangers! So it makes sense that as an F you trust your feelings—and are more likely to follow your heart.

Who Does the World See?

You've already discovered whether you're a T or an F and an S or an I. Here's the surprise: You probably show the world only one of these parts of your personality. Which one does everyone else see?

For each question, check the phrase that better describes you. If both responses fit you, choose the one that describes you more often.

Column A

1. I prefer to make a decision and then stick with it. ❏
2. I feel better after making a final decision. ❏
3. I like to finish projects. ❏
4. I don't like surprises—I'd rather have a "heads up." ❏
5. I enjoy making lists and checking off completed items. ❏
6. I'm more comfortable when things are planned out. ❏
7. I'm happier when things are settled. ❏

Column B

1. I'm game to adapt my decisions to whatever comes along. ❏
2. I feel better before making decisions. ❏
3. I like to start projects. ❏
4. I love surprises and last-minute changes. ❏
5. Even if I make a "to do" list, I usually end up ignoring it. ❏
6. I'd rather live spontaneously, taking whatever comes along! ❏
7. I like it when things are flexible. ❏

Scoring

If you checked more Column A responses, you're a **"J," OR JUDGER.**
As a **J,** you like things organized, and that includes decisions. Loose ends can drive you batty! You show the world whether you're a Thinker or a Feeler (since those are the things you base your judgments on).

If you checked more Column B responses, you're a **"P," OR PERCEIVER.**
P's don't mind so much when plans are up in the air or things are still left to be decided. In fact, you prefer spontaneity! You show the world whether you are a Sensor or an Intuitor (since those are the ways you gather perceptions).

The Results Are In!

Need a place to keep all your answers together in one spot? Ta-da! (You ask, we provide.) Use these pages to remember your scores— or even to share or compare them with friends!

Your room is a:
- ❏ Place of perfection
- ❏ Welcome retreat
- ❏ Creative work-in-progress

Your sleep style says you're:
- ❏ Quiet and reserved
- ❏ A good listener
- ❏ Shy and sensitive
- ❏ Outgoing and daring
- ❏ Social and easy to get along with
- ❏ Slow to trust

You are:
- ❏ A pessimist, who sees the glass as half empty
- ❏ An optimist, who sees the glass as half full

Your skills help you:
- ❏ Lead naturally
- ❏ Lead when needed
- ❏ Follow the leader

When it comes to competition, you're a:
- ❏ Sport
- ❏ Competitor
- ❏ Contender

When it comes to being perfect, you:
- ❏ Require perfection
- ❏ Want perfection
- ❏ Accept perfection

Your chance dance is a:
- ❏ Slow dance
- ❏ Fast dance

You're creatively a(n):
- ❑ Entertaining cat
- ❑ Storytelling cat
- ❑ Crafty cat

You're a personality Type:
- ❑ A
- ❑ B

Your self-image makes you:
- ❑ Catwalk confident
- ❑ Mirror avoidant

You learn best by:
- ❑ Listening
- ❑ Doing
- ❑ Seeing

You prefer to work out of your:
- ❑ Right brain
- ❑ Left brain

As a butterfly, you're:
- ❑ Natural
- ❑ Seasonal
- ❑ Social

Your career personality is:
- ❑ Mysterious
- ❑ Friendly
- ❑ Welcoming

We can depend on you being:
- ❑ Miss unpredictable
- ❑ Miss interdependent
- ❑ Miss independent

When you're way stressed, you're a:
- ❑ Diva
- ❑ Princess
- ❑ Queen

Your imagination leaves you with your:
- ❑ Feet on the ground
- ❑ Head in the clouds
- ❑ Feet in the clouds

And the four letters that describe you best:
- E or I ____
- S or N ____
- T or F ____
- J or P ____

The Big Picture

After completing all the quizzes and activities in this book, aren't you just dying for someone to ask you to describe who you are?! Why wait? Use this page to record what you've discovered about you. But this time, don't limit yourself to words—draw pictures, splash on color, or paste in things that represent the inner personality you've discovered. Do it your way!

....
....
....
....
....
....
....
....
....
....
....
....
....
....
....
....